Kaleidoscopic Skies

Ekta Daryani

CONTENTS

One day,
fires won't be
set alight by
dreams.

If only I had known
how time would change,
my sweet laughs would have shown
that my mind is deranged.
Come winter, the cold, harsh,
strenuous fear
of twisted pearls and indigo tears.

We're locked within iridescent chains of iron in this melded world of ice
and fire, hoping that the scorching flames will assuage the disasters
within our minds. Every night the sky is speckled with glimmering
pebbles, swirling around the stained glass of the mirror and entwining the
stars against cerulean catastrophes. It's a maze and the evil's eyes are
gleaming, mocking the world behind the glass as if this endless portal to
celestial vespertide thrives upon the sun lusted scrutiny of these creatures
we call humans. The fire seethes and strokes itself into a shape of a man
and it's the evil again, only this time, the reflections have set him alight
and he's cackling, drawing in screeching compendiums of each and every
speck of
what once was.
The light recedes and he is no longer there but our world is aflame.
The stillness of these shadows,
the abyss of these auras,
the wrenching twist in the very earth of the ground;
This world is lost at sea but the boats are still here, as if they were
waiting,
watching the clock,
as time twirled around a handle and the keys turned in the
locks.

I remember the rain;
the violet skies
like shaded hues
of dandelion embers.

I'll turn these epitaphs into eclipses,
for the idiosyncrasies of time
have overshadowed the moon and the sun.
This light will now flicker and fall,
setting candles ablaze as the sunset ignites.

Like silence, you speak and daisy smiles trace clocks made from
whispering moments, I;
am a knight in a series of storms that I see in your eyes, the ones that
you love;
in these streets where rain fell into life, and nothing in this war stops
them
from talking to
you;

sometimes the poet doesn't know the meaning of the words until
they are written.

We're made of fire, with minds so dire.
If you've crossed and are losing, safe but still choosing,
silver rays of dark
will send you to the show--
of rain,
of flames,
of perilous sparks.
We'll face the wrath of preyed foes, and superimpose
our hearts and our words;
these living ghosts.

Fireworks spin our footsteps;
this mindless noise ripples effervescence and the sunlight shines rays of
caramel on dreamt conversations.
Verse after verse we speak in iridescence,
and the sky can only hold
our silence.

Cobalt nights are engraved in violet;
they streak across the sky in twisted flares.
Emerald seas take in the words around them and arrows are the
nothingness, the beaming rays of obsidian starlight, meant to shatter the
blue and fall into dusk.
And in a heartbeat the quiet is the sound, the thrum of minds oppugning
the noise because dreams are infernos that we welcome into ourselves--
from the minutes twirling within seconds we have never let the bitter
snow know more than winter stars. Calls for home curse these walls and
they are met with startled laughter; framed against the dark we rise
towards this brilliance and luminous brightness collides.
We walk towards the rain.

Laughter tastes sweet on my tongue, like ice. Memories are stories
that start as ghosts and have you
met the silhouettes in your mind? They like to play tricks,
these tricks--
kaleidoscopic images press into the gravel of graphite markings. You
write, you write
but the pictures you have created come to life,
and on the bridgework of fading stars,
we are the war.

Darkness is a form of light.
Remember that,
before you ignite.

There's something about colors,
and the way they illuminate every ethereal verisimilitude;
the stars and the way they shade hues of
fire
when sequestered light
casts auroras
over the rain.

The dreamers are here, we're yours to fear.
We look around and change the world,
or burn it down and make it cold.
Through ink and words we
hold our knives;
of tragedy and sorrow,
they're our disguise.

Every moment, simply here,
our minds are captured on chalkboard walls, colliding against dreamt
keys.
We make sense from nonsense but never will we scribble our universe
in the same way as the mapmakers. No supernova can defy the infinity,
and no aurora will take ours away.

We counted to eight before the numbers danced along oceans and the
waves turned into fireworks.
We know it by heart, the stories of trembling illumination--
tasting salt, the moon rises against the sea and the sky lights up in jade.
You don't know these words,
and I painted along the lines in a conundrum. I wrote music that played
with time and
only uneven lines can tell the letters
that my eyes didn't color brushstrokes on your marks.

Golden leaves fall into place,
the world begins to paint its face.
We dance in the rain and
this laughter echoes off of the walls.
Steps of time, homes of our minds,
memories are the worlds within our words,
and as we taste blazing smiles on our lips,
our eyes take in the sound.

Two hundred and one thousand, five hundred and sixteen. When the
ineffable universe cascaded along its accretion, constellations formed
years, and just there, our hurricanes were apertures into the wildfires of
time.
This balance beam holds up infernos of metalloid verses;
Clocks beat chaos as glass was the gravity that held us down when our
uneven screams echoed off the walls.
We spin around future spheres and these seconds shape themselves into
moments, but we won't remember the blur,
because while our eyes take in the darkness, every now will
be an infinity.

We start from the ground, up.
Before: Intricate nighttime secrets were encased by ruby homes, as
we inked our own minds and painted ourselves with lustrous seas.
Come forward, see with your eyes, the lights that flickered on and
off.
Step a little closer, and look at the clock--
the handles were bent by
an arrow,
meant to draw pleas of rain with sidewalk chalk.
We were loved, but we did not love, and the eclipses hid our
shadows.
Now: Earthen gates lifted the petrichor and steps collided in an aria
of chorus. The scarlet walls crashed down and we built sapphire
ones instead; starlight clockwork mechanisms did not flare.
Our voices are on the ephemeris of scintillating beams and it is hard
to remember fluorescent goodbyes. But we made it through the
chaos and we erased our faces in favor of sketching our own eyes.
We once thought that silence would be our fate,
but that was before our spoken words
created a silhouetted slate.

One by one, the night;
it falls into the firestorm.
You walk into the stain of glass, but the way the ocean wove itself
within flames of gold does not begin.
When your paper lilted music speaks to itself, glimmering ink will
leave to talk to the silence.
Sunlight scintillates on the moon and spills within our minds, locked
against what we have spoken of, but when the time comes to say
these words they will have twisted--
One, two, one, two, counting won't bring back the sound, and on
this earth, it won't be found.
The painting gleams with iris flashes;
beneath this effervescent mess,
we hear our promise.
And we rebel against ourselves.

Shaking hands
leave cobalt seas
in their palms and
phantasmagorical enigmas
write dreams
by themselves.

But in the end, we are all picturesque paper dolls,
holding hands and letting go
as we all fall down
into the cacophonies of triturated dreams.

A road paved with night.
Two glimmering sunsets, chasing stars underneath stories.
Laughter. And rain.
And the notion of seaside moonlight writing constellations within
your home,
because at last, spoken words and timelines
didn't seem to look like reflections
after all.

Roses.
A knot in the sky, wringing
hands together--
and colors.
Emerald raindrops clung to the earth,
almost as if they were
coming home.

Indefinite ethereal catastrophes trace supernovas on your skin.
Voices echo in the starlight,
your veins are pulsing dreams and your words;
they speak.
It's fall in the apertures and the forests ink smiles on your face--
the world could never be more different
yet all the same.

And just in this one night,
we chased the world
and our minds,
for once,
spoke what we could not.
Look at the stars and breathe.
Reverberating against gleaming stories,
the symphonies silenced the moment,
and the aftermath of the light that we've known
dances rivers in the storm.

Made in the USA
Las Vegas, NV
26 November 2020